SERVING GOD'S PURPOSE IN YOUR GENERATION

by Dr. Mark Amoateng

Table of Contents

INTRODUCTION

"I'm ecstatic over what you say, like one

who strikes it rich"

(Psalms 119:162 MSG)

The Word of God is the manual God has given mankind to live by. With the truths revealed in the Scriptures, you excel in life. King David knew this blessed truth so when he heard God's Word, he rejoiced and was ecstatic like one who had struck it rich.

In every generation God has specific purposes, assignments and mandates for men to accomplish, and He looks for people who are available and willing to pursue and bring His predetermined counsel to fruition. There is a hungry child somewhere in the world right now, and God is looking for an available, prepared person to feed him or her. There are millions of souls all around the world who are unsaved, and God is looking for someone to seek and to save their immortal souls from eternal damnation.

You are born for a reason and you are alive for a cause. There is a definite reason why you are living at this time in human history. There is a reason why you live in that neighborhood and you are employed at your current workplace.

"And hath made of one blood all nations of men for to dwell on all the face of the earth, and hath determined the times before appointed, and the bounds of their habitation" (Acts 17:26 KJV).

Your times and bounds of habitation are appointed for a great goal. You are not a serendipitous event. Your coming into the world did not take God by surprise. Maybe it took your parents by surprise, but God was certainly not surprised; before the world began, you were on His mind. Borrowing the words of Mordecai, I can confidently tell you this: you are in the world for such a time like this to execute and finish a special mission.

"…and who knoweth whether thou art come to the kingdom for [such] a time as this?" (Esther 4:14 KJV).

You are a man or woman on a grand mission, and you have been packaged to fulfill it. Everything you will ever need is already provided for. The resources and the circumstances that are consistent with your mandate have been taken care of. All you have to do is to discover what you need to unleash that purpose on your generation.

In this masterpiece, you will discover how to discern that great purpose and the tools required for its execution. The fulfillment of the ages is upon you!

"…on whom the fulfillment of the ages has come" (1 Corinthians 10:11 NIV).

CHAPTER 1

SERVE YOUR GENERATION

The Scriptures are written for our example and admonition.

"Now all these things happened unto them for ensamples: and they are written for our admonition, upon whom the ends of the world are come" (1 Corinthians 10:11 KJV).

By studying and reading the Scriptures you will know what life is about, what you ought to do and how you must maximize your journey on earth.

King David was one of the men in the Scriptures who lived a full and fulfilled life. Using his life as a case study, let's glean precious truths about the purpose of existence.

YOU ARE HERE TO SERVE

"For David, after he had served his own generation by the will of God, fell on sleep, and was laid unto his fathers, and saw corruption" (Acts 13:36 KJV).

David's biography and life assignment is summarized in the verse above. David lived to serve his generation: it is as simple as that. King David did a lot and accomplished much but his whole purpose was to serve his generation. He lived for only one purpose--to serve his generation.

As it was for David, so it is for everyone. The reason why anyone is alive is to serve his or her generation. You are here to serve a generation. A whole generation is waiting on your service. At the end of your life God wants this to be true of you too. So, you put your name in the blank space below to complete the verse and discover how it will read.

"For _____, when he had served his own generation by the will of God, fell on sleep and was laid unto his fathers, and saw corruption."

Beloved, this must be your consciousness. It must be your passion to serve your generation. It must be all you dream and think of--serving your generation--because that is what life is about.

Now understand that you are here to serve and not to be served. Stop looking for who or what to serve you and start looking for who and where to serve.

You are not alive just to eat, marry, work, earn money, retire and go on vacations. You are alive to serve your generation. You eat, marry, work and earn money so that you can serve your generation. It is all a means to an end, not an end in itself. If you are ever asked why you are alive, your response should be 'to serve a generation'. Do you know why you can breathe? To serve your generation. Do you know why you own a car? To serve your generation. Do you know why you possess abilities and talents? To serve your generation.

EVEN JESUS CAME TO SERVE!

Friend, even Jesus who was the very son of God came into the world to serve. If anyone deserved to be served, I believe it was Jesus. He came from God and He was very God. His birth was miraculous and spectacular. He wielded and carried the very power that created the universe. He was the creator Himself to say the very least, yet read what He told His disciples:

"Just as the Son of Man did not come to be served, but to serve, and to give his life as a ransom for many" (Matthew 20:28 NIV).

This was how He lived every day. He was living among men as a servant. In another scripture He told his disciples that He was among them as one that serves:

"For whether [is] greater, he that sitteth at meat, or he that serveth? [is] not he that sitteth at meat? but I am among you as he that serveth" (Luke 22:27 KJV).

Jesus said He did not come into the world to sit but rather to serve. Don't be a 'sitter' in life. Instead, be a servant. Be like Jesus.

THE PROPHETS OF OLD WERE ALL SERVANTS!

The prophets and the fathers of old were all servants who served in their generation: **"It was revealed to them that they were not serving themselves but you, when they spoke of the things that have now been told you by those** who have preached the gospel to you by the Holy Spirit sent from heaven. Even angels long to look into these things" (1 Peter 1:12 NIV).

Noah was a servant. Abraham was a servant. Isaac, Jacob and his sons were all servants. Samuel and all the prophets of old were servants too. The scripture above said they did not serve themselves. So, they served but not themselves-- they served their generation.

APOSTLES OF THE LORD JESUS WERE SERVANTS

The Apostles of the early church were servants. Peter, who was the head apostle, referred to himself as a servant.

"Simon Peter, <u>a servant</u> and an apostle of Jesus Christ, to them that have obtained like precious faith with us through the

righteousness of God and our Saviour Jesus Christ" (2 Peter 1:1 KJV).

Paul the Apostle called himself a servant on many different occasions.

"Paul, <u>a servant of God</u>, and an apostle of Jesus Christ, according to the faith of God's elect, and the acknowledging of the truth which is after godliness" (Titus 1:1 KJV).

And again,

"For we preach not ourselves, but Christ Jesus the Lord; and <u>ourselves your servants</u> for Jesus' sake" (2 Corinthians 4:5 KJV).

LIFE IS ABOUT SERVING ONE ANOTHER

Someone may ask, "If everyone's purpose is to serve in life, then who will serve whom?" We serve one another. Life is all about serving one another.

"...serve one another in love" (Galatians 5:13 NLT).

In life we are all called to be servants, but we do not all serve in the same capacity. For example, the caterer serves the medical doctor by providing food so the latter will have the needed energy to work. On the other hand, the medical doctor takes care of the caterer's health so he or she can be well enough to make good meals.

YOUR GIFTS, TALENTS AND POTENTIAL WERE GIVEN TO YOU TO SERVE

Your talents and abilities were given to you to help fulfill your purpose, which is to serve your generation. The gifts you possess should be used to serve. They are not given to you to decorate your life or make you feel good. Peter the Apostle expressly told us the use of the gifts and talents

God gives to a person: TO SERVE OTHERS.

"Each one should use whatever gift <u>he</u> has received to serve others</u>, faithfully administering God's grace in its various forms" (1 Peter 4:10 NIV).

That is the purpose of your skills and potential. When you do not know this, you will abuse them. Many people abuse their gifts and talents because they are not aware of or very convinced about their purpose.

The first thing you must understand is that talents and gifts are given to servants; if you have a talent or a gift, then you are a servant. Secondly, the talents and skills you have are God's property. They are not yours. Because they are God's property, you will have to give account of them one day.

In the parable of the talents in the Gospel of Matthew, the Spirit of God brings these great truths to bear.

"Again, it will be like a man going on a journey, who called his <u>servants and entrusted his property to them</u>. To one he gave five talents of money, to another two talents, and to another one talent, each according to his ability. Then he went on his journey" (Matthew 25:14–15 NIV).

Use your talents as the owner of those talents demands because there is going to be a day of reckoning. Understand also that not using your talents is as bad as abusing them. In the parable of the talents, the man with one talent was punished for not using it.

"But the man who had received the one talent went off, dug a hole in the ground and hid his master's money" (Matthew 25:18 NIV).

Don't hide your talent in a hole. It is God's

property: value it and use it well.

GREATNESS IN LIFE IS CONNECTED TO YOUR SERVICE

Your service in this life and in God's kingdom determines your greatness. If you carry a servant's mentality you are on the path to greatness, and the reverse is true. Jesus Christ taught this truth to His disciples.

"But he that is greatest among you shall be your servant" (Matthew 23:11 KJV).

Again, He said:

"But ye [shall] not [be] so: but he that is greatest among you, let him be as the younger; and he that is chief, as he that doth serve" (Luke 22:26 KJV).

Believe the words of Jesus. The way to the top is the way down. Don't look to be served. Always look for opportunities to serve. In any setting you find yourself--whether it be in a relationship, at your workplace, in your church or family--look to serve.

To be the first, you must be the servant of all.

"Sitting down, Jesus called the Twelve and said, 'If anyone wants to be first, he must be the very last, and the servant of all'" (Mark 9:35 NIV).

Because Jesus came to the world to serve all of humanity, God has highly exalted and given Him a name and a position which is higher than any other in the universe.

"Wherefore God also hath highly exalted him, and given him a name which is above every name" (Philippians 2:9 KJV).

PREMATURE DEATH AND UNFULFILLED LIFE

"For when David had served God's

purpose in his own generation, he fell asleep; he was buried with his fathers and his body decayed" (Acts 13:36 NIV).

Premature death, according to God's Word, can be defined as dying before you finish your God-given purpose or assignment. It is believed that King David was at least seventy years old when he died. This is because he began his reign when he was thirty years old and was Israel's king for forty years, making a total of seventy years. However according to the above verse, the age at which King David died is beside the point: what matters the most is the fact that he finished and served God's purpose in his generation.

Jesus Christ died at the age of thirty-three and a half. This is quite a young age, but He lived a full life because He served God's purpose in His generation. I believe life is more about how well you live than how long you live.

One of the secrets of longevity is serving God's purpose in your generation. Any person serving his or her generation secures divine protection and preservation from all assaults of the devil. God needs such an individual here on earth, because if such a person leaves the earth before his or her time a vacuum will be created.

One confession you must make everyday is this: "I refuse to die until I have finished serving God's purpose in my generation." Again, always declare, "By the time I leave the world, the earth will know I have left and heaven will know I am coming."

CHAPTER 2

YOU WERE BORN FOR A PURPOSE

Everyone is created for a purpose and born for a reason. There is no one who was created by an accident. No one came to this planet without fitting in the grand design of God. You were born to fulfill a divine purpose.

When Jesus stood before Pontius Pilate, the Roman governor at the time of His trial, He was asked who He was. Pilate demanded to know whether Jesus was a king because that was part of the accusations against Him. In response, Jesus revealed His purpose for coming to the earth.

"Pilate therefore said unto him, Art thou a king then? Jesus answered, Thou sayest

that I am a king. **To this end was I born, and for this cause came I into the world,** that I should bear witness unto the truth. Every one that is of the truth heareth my voice" (John 18:37 KJV).

"To this end was I born," Jesus said, and for a divine cause He came into the world. Like Jesus, everyone is born for an end, and for a great cause we each exist. The purpose of Jesus' life was to bear witness to the truth. He knew exactly what His purpose was and fulfilled it to the maximum.

Jesus was a person on a mission. He was manifested for a specific purpose.

"...For this purpose the Son of God was manifested, that he might destroy the works of the devil" (1 John 3:8 KJV).

Like Jesus, you are here on a mission and you are manifesting for a purpose.

One individual who was totally convinced

that he was born and existed for a purpose was King David. One day he was sent by his daddy to deliver food to his brethren on the battlefield. When he arrived, he realized that a Philistine champion called Goliath was holding the whole nation of Israel and her armies to ransom. David began to sense the stirrings of purpose beckon him to take action. Something deep down within David told him he was born to fight giants. Something told young David that he existed to bring victory to a whole nation. And so, in response to the stirrings within him, he asked what was going on. His own elder brother Eliab scolded and criticized him for trying to pursue his purpose.

"And Eliab his eldest brother heard when he spake unto the men; and Eliab's anger was kindled against David, and he said, Why camest thou down hither? and with whom

hast thou left those few sheep in the wilderness? I know thy pride, and the naughtiness of thine heart; for thou art come down that thou mightest see the battle" (1 Samuel 17:28 KJV).

Beloved, when you decide to follow your purpose, you will be misunderstood, hindered and even insulted. That was exactly what happened to David. He was described as proud and naughty by his own brother. The very people who might oppose the pursuit of your God-given purpose and assignment might be those nearest and dearest to you, yet you must always be ready with the same response David gave: "Is there not a cause?"

"And David said, What have I now done? [Is there] not a cause?" (1 Samuel 17:29 KJV).

When David took care of his father's sheep no one criticized him, but when he made the attempt to fulfill the higher calling and purpose for his life he was challenged and even misunderstood. His brother Eliab thought he had only come to watch the battle.

Friend, you were not born to merely 'take care of a few sheep'; neither were you born to be a spectator in life as insinuated by Eliab. You must leave the small things of life and enter into the more significant God-given mandate for your life. The Eliabs of life will want you to live just to take care of some sheep. You are not here on earth to only work, marry and die. There is a higher cause. There is a higher purpose.

Tell the Eliabs of life that you came not to be a spectator of life but an active participant. Like David, you are not here to watch the battle: you came to end it. You came to kill the giant.

Paul the Apostle was another great personality who understood that he was alive for a purpose. He lived for that one singular purpose when he discovered it.

"…but [this] one thing [I do], forgetting those things which are behind, and reaching forth unto those things which are before" (Philippians 3:13 KJV).

When you truly discover purpose, you forget all other things and reach forward to its attainment and fulfilment. Apostle Paul was so sure and certain of his purpose to the extent that he knew when he had fully accomplished it.

"I have fought a good fight, I have finished [my] course, I have kept the faith" (2 Timothy 4:7 KJV).

Why do you get up every morning? Which cause are you living for? You are here for a purpose. Fulfill it.

YOU ARE BORN FOR GOD'S PURPOSE, NOT YOUR OWN

"Now when David had served God's purpose in his own generation, he fell asleep; he was buried with his ancestors and his body decayed" (Acts 13:36 NIV).

You are created to serve God's purpose like David, who served and fulfilled not his father's or mother's purpose but God's. Many people are fulfilling different purposes which are not God's.

Many people are consciously serving Satan's purpose whilst others are doing that unconsciously. There are many still who are neither fulfilling God's purpose nor the devil's purpose but their own purpose. I call this *Self-purpose*. Self-purpose is the purpose a person generates for himself or herself out of presumption. Whose purpose are you serving? Whose dream are you fulfilling? Are you even

25

fulfilling any purpose at all?

Your college degree, the house you own and the car you drive is not what I am not referring to as God's purpose. Anyone can buy a car or build a house whether they believe in the existence of God or not. Atheists graduate with degrees too! It is what you do with what you have, who you are and where you have been which determines whether you are serving God's purpose, Self-purpose or Satan's purpose.

HOW DO YOU SERVE GOD'S PURPOSE?

It is very simple to know when you are serving God's purpose. David was a man who served God's purpose, so we can learn how to do it from him. God had great pleasure in King David. He was actually referred to as a man after God's own heart. What made him a man after God's heart was simply the fact that he served

God's purpose. How did he do that? This is disclosed in the Bible verse quoted below:

"After removing Saul, he made David their king. He testified concerning him: 'I have found David son of Jesse a man after my own heart; <u>he will do everything I want him to do</u>" (Acts 13:22 NIV).

David was a man after God's own heart and a man who served God's purpose because he did everything God wanted him to do.

To serve God's purpose is to do what God wants you to do. If you do what you want to do, you are fulfilling self-purpose. If you do what the Satan wants you to do, you are serving Satan's purpose.

It is easy to become a man after God's heart. You must find out what He would have you do, then do it. That is how you become a man after God's heart.

HOW TO DISCOVER GOD'S PURPOSE

First of all, to know what God wants you to do you must have a heart that seeks to know what God wants. Your heart must desire to know this. When it is truly in your heart to know what God wants for you, you will pray the prayer of Paul the Apostle: "Lord, what will you have me do?"

"And he trembling and astonished said, <u>Lord, what wilt thou have me to do?</u> And the Lord [said] unto him, Arise, and go into the city, and it shall be told thee what thou must do" (Acts 9:6 KJV).

That was Paul the Apostle's first prayer after he heard the voice of the Lord. Many people have never prayed such a prayer. I strongly believe it should be the prayer of every person.

Paul prayed and God responded, instructing him to arise and go into the city; there, it would be told him what he must do. When you pray this prayer now you might not be directed to a city, but there are two basic places I believe you will be directed to.

1.   THE WORD OF GOD – THE SCRIPTURES

God's Word contains God's will for your life. When you study and understand the Scriptures by the help of the Holy Spirit you will discern what God wants you to do, for it is written of you 'in the volume of the book'. The will of God for your life is revealed in the Scriptures. Jesus declared that His purpose was written 'in the volume of the book'. The will of God for His life was enshrined therein:

"Then said I, Lo, I come (in the volume of the book it is written of me,) to do thy will, O God" (Hebrews 10:7 KJV).

The prophet Isaiah also said 'the vison of all

are like words written in a book'. I believe he meant the vision of God for your life can be found in the Scriptures.

"And the vision of all is become unto you as the words of a book that is sealed..." (Isaiah 29:11 KJV).

Child of God, I believe that before the foundations of the world God thought about you and wrote of you 'in the volumes of the book'. You were created in Christ Jesus to accomplish and do good works which were already ordained for you to walk in.

"For we are his workmanship, created in Christ Jesus unto good works, which God hath before ordained that we should walk in them" (Ephesians 2:10 KJV).

2. CHECK WITHIN YOUR HEART

Secondly, you discover what God wants you

to do or God's purpose for your life by checking what He communicates to your heart. The truth is that God's will and counsels for your life are written in your heart. His eternal law and decision are within your heart. That is where God dwells. Read what David wrote:

"I delight to do thy will, O my God: yea, thy law [is] within my heart" (Psalms 40:8 KJV).

The will of God is encoded in your heart. You must learn to decode it. All the issues and happenings of life emanate and stem from the heart of man.

"Keep thy heart with all diligence; for out of it [are] the issues of life" (Proverbs 4:23 KJV).

Every will of God is in your heart. Many people are waiting for a dramatic vision or an angel to appear with bright lights before they believe what God has been telling them all this while. You do not need to be spooky to know the will of God.

The first intimations for Moses to walk and fulfill God's purpose were discovered in his heart. When Moses turned forty years of age, his purpose entered into his heart. Suddenly he had a passion for the people he was born to deliver from slavery.

"And when he was full forty years old, <u>it came into his heart</u> to visit his brethren the children of Israel" (Acts 7:23 KJV).

Sometimes the voice of God can be communicated to you as desire or passion in your heart. When you spend time in prayer, fasting and meditating on God's Word, the voice of God in your heart becomes clearer and easy to perceive; then you are able to discern God's purpose for your life.

CHAPTER 3

INTEGRITY OF HEART AND SKILLFULNESS OF HANDS

We have used King David as a case study of how to successfully fulfill and serve God's purpose in your generation. I believe that by now, you have discovered what it means to serve God's purpose. To serve God's purpose, simply find out what He wants you to do and do it.

In this chapter and the succeeding ones, we will concentrate on how to do what God wants you to do effectively and efficiently. It is not enough to do what God wants you to do: it must be done very well. He is God and He deserves to receive the best from you.

Let's examine how King David served his generation. What was he supposed to do? How did he do it? In Psalms 78, we are given the answers to these questions:

"He chose David also his servant, and took him from the sheepfolds: From following the ewes great with young <u>he brought him to feed Jacob his people</u>, and Israel his inheritance. So he fed them according to the <u>integrity of his heart</u>; and guided them by the <u>skillfulness of his hands</u>" (Psalms 78:70–72 KJV).

King David's assignment, mandate or purpose was to feed Jacob or Israel, the people of God. He was to guide and lead them according to God's dictates and plans. Don't forget David was a king, so as a king he was the leader of the entire nation of Israel. As their leader he did two things - he fed the people and guided them. The will of

God for King David was to feed and guide the nation of Israel. Feeding and guiding the people are the two main assignments of all God-ordained leaders.

A closer look at the verses above will reveal to us that King David did not do this work anyhow. He possessed two great qualities with which he served God's purpose in his generation. What were they? Integrity of heart and skillfulness of hands.

Beloved, what made David become a man after the heart of God was not merely feeding and guiding Israel. There were many other kings before and after him who were not men after the heart of God. What made him different was the integrity of his heart and the skillfulness of his hands. The quality of your 'heart and hands' will determine whether you serve God's purpose fully in your generation or not.

These two qualities must work together. You cannot sacrifice one for the other. They are two great essentials in the fulfillment of destiny. Actually, in any field of life whether concerning career development, ministry work, marriage, parenting or sports, these two qualities must be present in order to stand out.

Have you ever seen someone with great skills--well educated, intelligent, eloquent, very skillful at what he or she does--but who also lacks integrity? This situation is very common in the sports world. You will find very skillful and talented players: as long as they are in a game, their team is sure of a win. But they might have serious character flaws and cannot be trusted. They can make the news in two ways; either they score the winning goal or they bring a serious scandal on the whole team.

In the Scriptures a story is told of Saul, the

first king of Israel, who was tormented by an evil spirit because God had left him. His servants said that if a harp was played the evil spirit would leave him alone, which meant they needed an individual who could play the harp. I believe there were thousands of people who could play the harp in the nation of Israel, so who would they choose for this job? They would have to look out for certain qualities. Let's consider the criteria for their selection.

"Saul's servants said to him, Behold, an evil spirit from God torments you. Let our lord now command your servants here before you to find a man <u>who plays skillfully</u> on the lyre; and when the evil spirit from God is upon you, he will play it, and you will be well. Saul told his servants, Find me a man who plays well and bring him to me. One of the young men said, I have seen a son of Jesse

the **Bethlehemite** <u>who plays skillfully</u>, a <u>valiant man, a man of war, prudent</u> in speech and eloquent, an attractive person; and the Lord is with him" (1 Samuel 16:15–18 AMP).

First of all, they needed someone who was very skillful in playing the harp. They searched for someone who could play really well. David was not at the palace at that time but his skill spoke for him. He was known as the best harp player in the whole nation. David had the skillfulness of hands.

Yet that was not in enough. They had to look for other qualities. Skillfulness of hands is not enough to work in a palace. Integrity of heart must also be present. David was prudent which means he was wise and sensible. He knew how to carry himself in the palace. In addition, he was very bold. He is described as 'a valiant man and a man of war'. He also had a likable personality which was a function of his integrity of heart. David needed skillfulness of hands and integrity of heart to enter King Saul's presence.

When Moses had to appoint elders and rulers to help him feed and lead God's people in the wilderness, he looked for these same two qualities: integrity of heart and skillfulness of hands.

"Moreover thou shalt provide out of all the people able men, such as fear God, men of truth, hating covetousness; and place [such] over them, [to be] rulers of thousands, [and] rulers of hundreds, rulers of fifties, and rulers of tens" (Exodus 18:21 KJV).

He chose able men (skillfulness of hands) and men who feared God, men of truth who hated covetousness (integrity of heart).

These same qualities were looked out for in the New Testament when leaders and workers were needed in the church. When the Apostles had to appoint men to help in the serving of tables and the distribution of food, they did not just go for either skillfulness of hand or integrity of heart: they sought men who had both qualities.

"Wherefore, brethren, look ye out among you seven <u>men of honest report, full of the Holy Ghost and wisdom,</u> whom we may appoint over this business" (Acts 6:3 KJV).

The men appointed were men of honest report and wise--integrity of heart. And of course, they had the ability to distribute food.

Paul the Apostle, in his first letter to Timothy, set the standard for appointing and selecting bishops or overseers. In his criteria, these same two qualities surfaced: integrity of heart and skillfulness of hands.

"Here is a trustworthy saying: If anyone sets his heart on being an overseer, he desires

a noble task. Now the overseer must be above reproach, the husband of but one wife, <u>temperate, self-controlled, respectable, hospitable, able to teach</u>" (1 Timothy 3:1–2 NIV).

An overseer had to be able to teach (skillfulness of hands) and be respectable, self-controlled, hospitable, sober and patient (integrity of heart).

Beloved, if you must serve God's purpose in your generation, you must do so with the skillfulness of your hands and the integrity of your heart. Pursue and develop both, and you will be a man after God's own heart.

Dr. Mark Amoateng

CHAPTER 4

THE INTEGRITY OF HEART

I n the previous chapter we identified two great necessities for the fulfilment of one's purpose and destiny. In this chapter, we turn our attention to one of them.

INTEGRITY OF HEART

"So he fed them according to the <u>integrity of his heart</u>…" (Psalms 78:72 KJV).

What does the phrase or expression 'integrity of heart' really mean? The Hebrew word used for *integrity* is the word *t^om*, which means 'completeness or to be complete'. Integrity of heart talks about the completeness of one's character.

There are several components of one's heart which can classify it as a heart of integrity. We will consider several scriptures to ascertain the components of 'integrity of heart'.

Firstly, let's look at the qualifications used for selecting rulers in the time of Moses.

"Moreover thou shalt provide out of all the people able men, such as fear God, men of truth, hating covetousness; and place [such] over them, [to be] rulers of thousands, [and] rulers of hundreds, rulers of fifties, and rulers of tens" (Exodus 18:21 KJV).

From the above verse we identify three components of integrity of heart:

1. The fear of God

2. Truthfulness or sincerity

3. Hating covetousness

Secondly, let's take a look at the characteristics of David which qualified him to serve in King Saul's palace.

"Then answered one of the servants, and said, Behold, I have seen a son of Jesse the Bethlehemite, [that is] cunning in playing, and a mighty valiant man, and a man of war, and prudent in matters, and a comely person, and the LORD [is] with him" (1 Samuel 16:18 KJV).

We identify two additional components of integrity of heart from this verse:

1. Valiance/boldness/courage

2. Prudence

Next, we look at the mode of selection in the days of the Apostles.

"Wherefore, brethren, look ye out among you seven men of honest report, full of the Holy Ghost and wisdom, whom we may appoint over this business" (Acts 6:3 KJV).

We discover two more constituents of

integrity of heart:

1. Honest report

2. Wisdom

And finally, we examine Paul the Apostle's benchmark for choosing overseers.

"Now the overseer must be above reproach, the husband of but one wife, temperate, self-controlled, respectable, hospitable, able to teach, not given to drunkenness, not violent but gentle, not quarrelsome, not a lover of money. He must manage his own family well and see that his children obey him with proper respect. (If anyone does not know how to manage his own family, how can he take care of God's church?). He must not be a recent convert, or he may become conceited and fall under the same judgment as the devil. He must also have a good reputation with outsiders, so that

he will not fall into disgrace and into the devil's trap" (1 Timothy 3:2–7 NIV).

We can establish twelve vital elements of the integrity of heart from this passage of scripture:

1. Above reproach
2. Temperate/vigilant
3. Self-controlled
4. Respectable
5. Hospitable
6. Not violent but gentle
7. Not given to wine
8. Not a lover of money
9. Not quarrelsome
10. Good manager
11. Good reputation
12. Not promiscuous (the meaning of the expression 'the husband of one wife')

From the above lists, you will discover that 'integrity of heart' has several pieces and ingredients. These traits of integrity are not mere gifts you receive overnight or in an instant. We must endeavor to develop and increase in them.

It is noteworthy to say that integrity of heart is doing your very best to fulfill the assignment and mandate God has ordained for your life. When all is said and done, can you say you did your best to serve God's purpose?

I believe this prayer of David helped him to develop integrity of heart, and it will help you too:

"Search me, O God, and know my heart: try me, and know my thoughts: And see if [there be any] wicked way in me, and lead me in the way everlasting" (Psalms 139:23–24 KJV).

CHAPTER 5

THE SKILLFULNESS OF HANDS

In this chapter we will talk about the second quality needed to serve God's purpose in your generation, and that is the *skillfulness of hands*.

"...and guided them by the skilfulness of his hands" (Psalms 78:72 KJV).

The expression 'skillfulness of hands' refers to aptitude, prowess or competence. It simply refers to the ability to do something well. The above verse then means that David guided and led with expertise. He was a master at what he did.

Beloved, you cannot serve God's purpose in your generation without skillfulness of hands.

49

Having a good heart to do something is not enough qualification. For example, if you sat in an airplane and the pilot announced to everyone, "Hello, I am a young man who has integrity of heart. I am an honest person who is also kindhearted and I have a strong desire to fly a plane. But I have no skill. Actually, I am yet to apply to flight school". I am very certain of what you would do--you would leave the plane right away! You would not want anyone to experiment or toy with your precious life. The truth is that when you have integrity of heart but lack skillfulness of hands, you will be liked but not useful. You may have very good intentions, but you will accomplish nothing.

In the same vein, whatever your assignment or purpose in life is, you must develop the right skill and depth of understanding in that area to efficiently discharge your mandate. Your ability, knowledge, intelligence and insight in your scope of endeavor reveal the skillfulness of your hands.

There are several depths of skill development. The first stage is when you only have a basic understanding of the matter at hand. Next is the stage where you are said to possess aptitude, which is the actual ability to do something. At the first stage, you understand the basics but that does not mean you can do the work involved. At the second stage you can actually get the job done. The final stage is the stage of mastery and expertise. At this stage, you have developed dexterity and excellence at what you do. You show a high level of competence. Everyone can say you are good at what you do.

This was what was said about David. He was a cunning player of the harp. David was an excellent musician.

"One of the young men spoke up, 'I know

someone. I've seen him myself: the son of Jesse of Bethlehem, an excellent musician'" (1 Samuel 16:18 MSG).

David's soldiers and men of war were said to be skillful and dexterous. They were so skilled, they could use both hands to throw stones.

"Now these [are] they that came to David to Ziklag, while he yet kept himself close because of Saul the son of Kish: and they [were] among the mighty men, helpers of the war. [They were] armed with bows, <u>and could use both the right hand and the left in [hurling] stones and [shooting] arrows out of a bow,</u> [even] of Saul's brethren of Benjamin" (1 Chronicles 12:1–2 KJV).

Daniel and his friends were men who served God's purpose in their generation. The Scriptures reveal that they were skillful men.

"Children in whom [was] no blemish, but

well favoured, and skilful in all wisdom, and cunning in knowledge, and understanding science, and such as [had] ability in them to stand in the king's palace, and whom they might teach the learning and the tongue of the Chaldeans" (Daniel 1:4 KJV).

There are different skills you might need in the fulfilment of your assignment, and based on your field of assignment you might require different skills in different measures. There are social skills, communication skills, leadership skills, artistic skills, musical skills, workplace skills, spiritual skills and many more you must develop relative to your field of concentration.

There are three main ways of acquiring skills. Skills can be inherited, taught and imparted.

King David was taught the skill of war by God. A human personality can also teach you a skill.

"He teacheth my hands to war, so that a bow of steel is broken by mine arms" (Psalms 18:34 KJV).

Bezaleel received an impartation with the skill of craftsmanship. He was not taught by a man.

"See, I have called by name Bezaleel the son of Uri, the son of Hur, of the tribe of Judah: And I have filled him with the spirit of God, in wisdom, and in understanding, and in knowledge, and in all manner of workmanship" (Exodus 31:2–3 KJV).

No matter what the source of your skills is, you must keep developing and improving upon them. Your generation deserves your best and God also deserves your best. Make up your mind to be a lifelong learner. Don't just do enough to get by. Grow and expand into mastery and preeminence. Read, study, train, yield yourself to mentorship and receive impartations to develop your skills. Also, be willing to embrace change and new technological advancements.

Most of the time, skills are developed in obscurity. David became a master at playing the harp in the bush where no one but his father's sheep was listening. You must master the sets of skillfulness consistent with your calling and mandate when no one is watching. Your private preparations will produce public exploits and excellence if you do not give up.

Child of God, are you training yourself or developing skills necessary for serving God's purpose in your generation? Maybe you can sing, is it your best? Maybe you can preach, is it your best? Maybe you can write, paint or lead; is that your best? Whatever you can do, is it your best? Stretch yourself, push yourself to the limit. Do everything in your power to develop the skills needed to live and fulfill your destiny and purpose in grand style.

Finally, I would like to encourage you not to despise any skill you possess right now. It might look like you have been given just one talent whilst others have received two or even five. Can I tell you something? What you have is enough. Develop it. All Moses had was an old shepherd's rod, yet it was enough to deliver a whole nation. That little rod swallowed serpents, divided the Red Sea and worked many amazing wonders.

Friend, now that you know these things you have no excuse to disappoint your generation and your Maker.

I believe it shall be written of you, "Now when **(YOUR NAME)** had served God's purpose in his own generation, he fell asleep; he was buried with his fathers and his body decayed" (Acts 13:36 NIV). Shalom!

Made in the USA
Coppell, TX
19 January 2023